T0372188

LET'S FIND LEVERS

by Wiley Blevins

raintree
a Capstone company — publishers for children

YOU USE IT TO LIFT THINGS.
YOU USE IT TO MOVE THINGS.

Do you know what it is? You probably see one wherever you go! It's a lever. A lever is a bar or rod. It rests on a point. Let's go on a hunt to find these simple machines!

GO UP.
GO DOWN.

Push your feet up
off the ground.
A see-saw is a lever.

It moves you UP and DOWN at the PLAYGROUND.

BAM! HIT THAT BALL.

Watch it soar. A bat is a lever that moves a ball fast and far.

CUT A PIECE OF PIZZA.

Hold it on your fork. Lift and move it to your mouth. Repeat!

A FORK IS A LEVER THAT HELPS YOU EAT.

LOOK AT THIS BUG!

It's so small. How will you pick it up? Use tweezers gently. **THAT'S ALL!**

CRUNCHY LEAVES COVER THE GROUND.

What will you do? Grab a rake. It's a long lever.

HOW MANY BIG LEAF PILES WILL YOU MAKE?

PEDAL, PEDAL, PEDAL.

But how will you stop?
Squeeze the bike's brakes.
That's all it takes!

THESE LEVERS STOP THE BIKE FROM MOVING.

CLEAR A SNOWY PATH.

Use two hands on the shovel's handle to push and lift the snow.

THE HANDLE IS A LEVER. ISN'T THAT CLEVER?

LIFT. POP. TUG.

This tin has a lever to lift off the lid. The cat sniffs and miaows.

THE TIN HOLDS ITS
FAVOURITE
FOOD!

SWEEP. SWEEP. SWEEP.

Move that dirt away. A broom gets the job done!

HOORAY!

It's DARK IN HERE!

No problem! Flip a switch. It is a lever.

MOVE IT UP. THE LIGHTS GO ON. MOVE IT DOWN. THE LIGHTS GO OFF.

EVEN YOUR BODY HAS LEVERS.

Where? Your arms and legs! They help you move.

YOU USE THEM TO HOLD AND LIFT THINGS TOO.

HERE'S A LEVER TO TRIM YOUR FINGERNAILS.

Nail clippers hold
the nail in place.
Now squeeze . . .

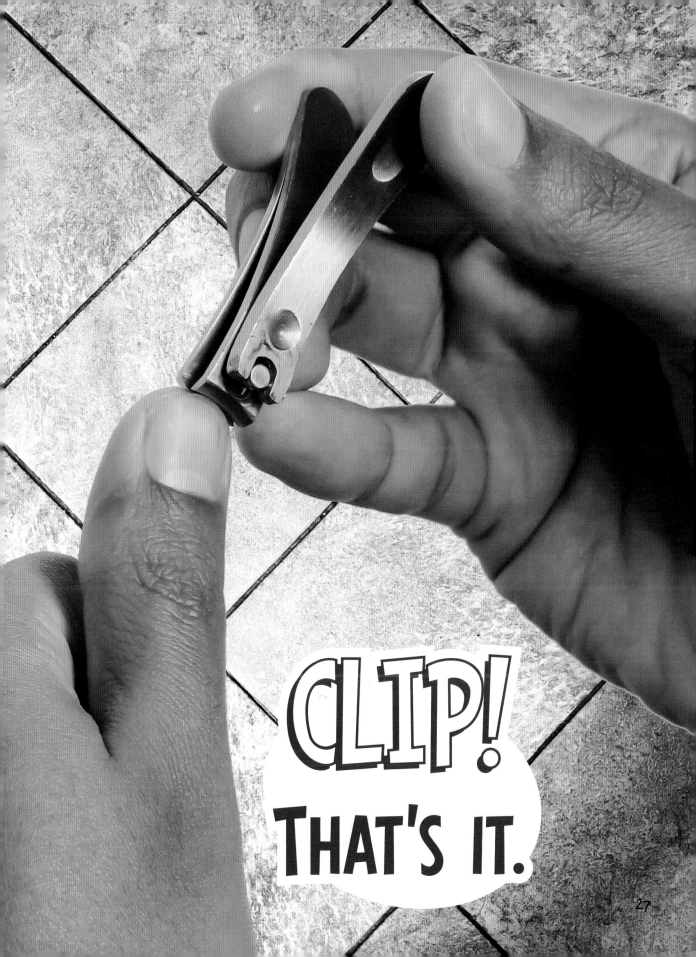

CLIP! THAT'S IT.

BIRDS HAVE LEVERS!

Do you know where?
Here's a clue.

THE BIRD USES IT TO HOLD ITS FOOD!

tweezers

fork

tin lid

rake

nail
clippers

bike brake

bat

light
switch

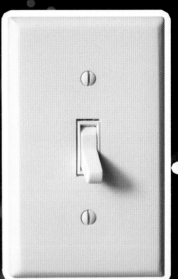

arms and legs

see-saw

broom

shovel

bird beak

Raintree is an imprint of Capstone Global Library Limited, a company incorporated in England and Wales having its registered office at 264 Banbury Road, Oxford, OX2 7DY – Registered company number: 6695582

www.raintree.co.uk
myorders@raintree.co.uk
Copyright © Capstone Global Library Limited 2022

ISBN 978 1 3982 0499 7 (hardback)
ISBN 978 1 3982 0500 0 (paperback)

Edited by Erika Shores
Designed by Kyle Grenz
Media Researcher: Tracy Cummins
Production by Spencer Rosio
Originated by Capstone Global Library Ltd
Printed and bound in India

Image Credits
iStockphoto: aldomurillo, 4–5, CasarsaGuru, 18–19, cglade, 10–11, dendong, 30 top right, FatCamera, 2–3, 24–25; Shutterstock: ArtFamily, 31 bottom left, Bokic Bojan, 26–27 background, Chalermpon Poungpeth, 8–9, clarst5, 31 bottom right, gennady, 30 top left, Goran Kuzmanovski, 30 middle left, Hurst Photo, 31 top right, Karel Gallas, 28–29, kdshutterman, 31 middle left, Lane V. Erickson, Cover, MARGRIT HIRSCH, 30 middle right, Mikhail Azarov, 16–17, MrVander, Design Element, Mtsaride, 31 top left, Olivier Le Queinec, 22–23, PONGNARET PALAMON, 26–27, Sergey Novikov, 14–15, Sergiy Kuzmin, 31 middle right, SHINPANU, 30 bottom left, sirtravelalot, 6–7, struna, 20–21, Suzanne Tucker, 12–13, Vereshchagin Dmitry, 31 bottom middle, Winai Tepsuttinun, 30 bottom right

British Library Cataloguing in Publication Data
A full catalogue record for this book is available from the British Library.

FIND OUT MORE ABOUT SIMPLE MACHINES BY CHECKING OUT THE WHOLE SERIES!